GW00568262

Gallery Books
Editor: Peter Fallon

ERRIS

Seán Lysaght

ERRIS

Gallery Books

Erris
is first published
simultaneously in paperback
and in a clothbound edition
on 7 November 2002.

The Gallery Press
Loughcrew
Oldcastle
County Meath
Ireland

© Seán Lysaght 2002

ISBN 1 85235 325 2 (*paperback*)
     1 85235 326 0 (*clothbound*)

A CIP catalogue record for this book
is available from the British Library.

The Gallery Press acknowledges the financial assistance
of An Chomhairle Ealaíon / The Arts Council, Ireland,
and the Arts Council of Northern Ireland.

Contents

Lines for a New House *page* 9

PART ONE
  Erris 13
  Luftmensch 14
  These Islands 15
  A Note from Greece 16
  The Gulf Stream 18
  Translation without an Original 19
  The Queen of Cliara 20
  Achill 21
  Greenshank 22
  Corncrake 24
  Tom the Tree 25
  Birdwatching 27
  Limerick
    1 A SIGN OF PEACE 28
    2 IN WEST LIMERICK 29
    3 RIVER-TOWN 30
    4 A STONE'S THROW 31
    5 A TRIP TO THE CAPITAL 32
    6 EEL-BOYS 33
    7 THE BOOKS IN MY ROOM 34
    8 HOME 35
  Flieger Hartmann 36
  Two Sculptures by Gerald Müller
    1 DOLPHIN BARGE 38
    2 AFRICA BARGE 40
  Gale Warning 42
  Horses at Corratowick 43
  The Helmet of Messapus 45
  Knock/Stansted 51
  Furze in Wind 52
  Summer 53
  Other Forms 54

The Previous Owner 55
A Souvenir 56
Bertra 60

PART TWO
    To Connacht 65

Two Goodbyes 92

Notes and Acknowledgements 94

Lines for a New House

Man and woman took this place
from the lark's song and the worm's peace
that in their time the heart would know
the lark above and the worm below.

PART ONE

Erris

When the first seal spoke in that language she mastered,
the whole barony swam in the lens of her eye.
They heard the seal's cries as the cries of their own kind,

so they tried naming the heathers, and the strange fish
they found turning speechlessly in the net's cradle.
But there was still that sky that wouldn't stay the same

and too many hills scarcely deserving their names
and, besides, what use to you will that ever be?
The seals deserted with the running shoal of tide

like weather that refused to pose for the painter,
and the tongue writhed out of the mouth in its struggle
with visa applications and subsidy forms.

The eel was finally free of folklore to cross
the shorn meadow on its way to the sea. The stoat
hid from the haymakers. The one-eyed deity

abandoned the mountains and came down their aerials
more reliably than when, in the high places,
the hilltop fires lit their stoops and flickering faces.

Luftmensch

The pooka, or the boody man,
is a *Luftmensch* — didn't you know
that he couldn't be traced
the day they all ran after the rainbow?

Like Chagall's lovers,
he flies through empty space
and still haunts the innocents
who married into the place.

These Islands

The Great Blasket, Beginish, Teeraght,
Inishtooshkert, Inishvickillaun, and Inis na Bró.
Tomás had seen them all before he started school

where the teacher introduced the map in English:
'Great Britain is over here, and this is where you live,
in Ireland. *Abraigí anois é*: Ireland.'

A Note from Greece

I have met them again, those strong Blasket boatmen,
pulling through the waves of charted history
on their way to Salamis or Marathon,

the whole crew intent, as Ó Croimhthain was,
on selling the best lobsters to a sour Athenian
cook. He was, as usual, bemused by the tourists

taking pictures from the back of the hydrofoil.
They even knew his name. 'Tomás! Tomás!'
they shouted, as if he had the time, as he toiled

towards the place where heartless powers meet
on the sea's glittering stage, and him well-oiled
from the bottles of Belgian beer stowed at his feet.

Men like him are happiest in the Aegean
as they supply the seafood bars, and keep
the ferries running smoothly according to plan.

Still you can't help being tempted to translate
into your own language, and so you try it on
as Achilles to Achill, Antigone to a Taig,

the Cyclops to Caochán. As proud as the day-trippers
with their fancy cameras, you also want to take
your own version of the island into your shutters,

and waste your time with the photos we all know.
Why stifle the day with antique letters?
On Delos, there's a theatre sacred to Apollo.

In ruins now, today it's full of song.
The crested lark speaks the language of the stones,
in tune with the lizard and the mullein among

the lines of ancient seating. I listen to a bird
in flight above the backward crab of tradition.
She forgets the old ordeal of those islanders

in the exile of their winter, the vigil of their night.
Now her voice is rising over the visitor
who's shadowed by her song of Periclean light.

The Gulf Stream

for Derek Walcott

On an instinct not to be denied
the eel-fry leave your ocean, Master,
and swim homing into my childhood

where I lived near the teeming river.
I have gathered enough at low tide
to be called back to the open coast

you save from freezing by your cadence.
One of your logs, lying on Cross Strand
with its delicate frills of bivalves,

was delivered from your epic island.
Those little hangers-on were like sails
for a thinnest fleet that the shoreman

raises now for his own occasion
as he floats that log and trusts the waves
to lift him in the sea's true scansion.

Translation without an Original

One man moving among the walls
of ruined houses; no war,
no fire, no famine either in his speech.
Just man, blethering man, and stone.

Oh, he has lived, of course.
He built walls in his own time
and drank when he was paid for them.
And there was a deeper sanction:

he bowed to an altar, he moved
through years of bewildered feeling.
But now he's perfected within
his own cantankerous nature.

As a man moves among the ruined
walls, stone keeps its shape as stone.
It's the man who won't obey.
He has always something else to say.

The Queen of Cliara

after Goethe

The pirate queen of Cliara
prized that golden cup
her dying lover left her
as he gave his spirit up.

Her kinsmen felt with envy
that each time it was filled
she drank to honour Henry,
an Englishman they'd killed.

They courted her with plunder,
with gold and Spanish wine.
She toasted their performance
with the cup every time.

After years of this she said
she'd make her choice today
and took the chalice with her
on a raid across the bay.

'If there's any man who fancies
he could spend a life with me,
let him get this token back
from the bottom of the sea.'

So she threw it overboard
and they watched their chances fade
with the cup sinking steadily
into the cold sea's shade.

Achill

Tradition has it that Achilles rested here
in a small cottage after his Trojan labours.
No one knows exactly where. The sea-breezes scour
the open land and eradicate the memory
of how he stood before his glamorous trireme
with his hero's crest.
                              Then, he put on pampooties
as he went to help the local men unloading.

His gold helmet was put above the mantelpiece
to gather ten years' dust.
                              It became the story
of how a local man called Harry O'Deasy
came back from England unannounced. He found
his farm run down, his dog neglected, his best
cattle sold — and so on. Of course you know the rest.

Greenshank

The sight came to a few birdmen
and that on a lucky day
when, out of the Hebrides,
a greenshank alighted

in a vast bay in the west.
It was restored to the guidebook
they thought they had lost it from.
Although the glare

was outlandish
the bird went scything
in those waters
and was nothing anyone could compare

it to, not even its *teu, teu, teu,*
when it left. No,
that was their loneliness
in the small end of the telescope

where they're all crowded in
with the whole of Sutherland,
and those summer pilgrims,
Desmond and Maimie.

The god they honoured
was a speck in the sky
to keep faith in
even as it disappears.

It was too busy feeding
to see the shoreline
sparkling at its feet,
and again it fled the story

of its autumn flight
as the *laidhrín* of another
language. In Whiddy
it was as clean as its own whistle.

Corncrake

This spring the corncrake
signalled its lonely morse
for a love-pledge broken.
Its voice became remorse,

the corncrake taking the blame
for its virtual disappearance.
'I wasn't strong enough,' it said.
'I wasn't committed to endurance.'

Last night we listened at the fields
and missed the pleading sound.
The bird of passage had moved
from the faithless ground

and left a silent iris.
Somewhere else its grief
to another flower tonight
will call its petals soft, its season brief.

Tom the Tree

Coming from a place with no trees
he had this fixation with wood.
'Now riddle me this,' he said.
'I'm the boat's gunwale. I'm the hull's wattle.
The keel is my leg. The oar is my rib. What am I?'
And he whirled the leaves of his tattered coat above
      the sea thrift,
calling to the dunes as he ran,
'A tree! A tree! A tree!',
as dark as the swallows he watched
dipping under the door of his mother's henhouse.
He was happiest in that gloom
where the birds fluttered at a roof beam above him.

He was a good man to foot turf, but not to cut.
He got distracted down there
where the ground collapsed under bog-oak,
the feet of giant trees that freaked him
in their stride across his mind
and, eventually, these monsters
surrounded him in the grounds of St Mary's.
The vast chestnuts writhed in the wind.
Their bony fingers called to him,
and his torment seemed blind
until the nurse finally realized,
'There now, *a leanbh*, sure it's only trees.'

The time in there did him more harm than good.

After they discharged him
he told his riddles to the logs on the shore,
or sang them songs with the slow drum of the waves,
and then one day
he found an oar that nobody remembered,
scuffed and battered from the surf.

This oar became his tree to measure gables with,
to outdo any rick of turf or hay
at full stretch above him.
He could even match the span of tide at the pier
if he held the oar like a priest holding the host.

'The oar is my rib,' he shouted
as he passed with the oar on his shoulder,
and someone shouted back,
'Why don't you get God to make you a woman, Tomás?'

The day he left, on the road to Bangor,
you'd think that someone would have wondered
why a man walked inland carrying an oar.
One man said, 'We've no oats for threshing yet,'
and watched him going away from the sea,
but he didn't stop him.

So he walked all day until he came
to where trees grow in a little glen between the eskers.
Rabbits were grazing there but they fled
when his approaching shape darkened the pasture.
He leaned his oar against a hawthorn
big enough to accept him.
It had an old woman's skin
with a mossy crotch at the fork.
On this foothold he levered himself
into the green stillness.
Then, suddenly, his legs shot down
to join the branches.
His trousers and socks became leaves.

Birdwatching

A bird on the ebbing tide
asserts its right
to be identified.

Limerick

I A SIGN OF PEACE

A peregrine sallies from the cathedral spire
and glides to the corner of the sky's page. Then
it works its strong wings rapidly along a line.

I feel the skein of history between us,
where a browsing deer hears the first strokes of the axe
in Cratloe, then runs off from Dunraven's beagles,

to be captured by her ladyship's aquarelle.
Gate-lodge and gate are still there in many places
to mark the passage of hunters and painters

when a falcon's flight commanded empty spaces.
Now the needle of a plane pulls its double thread
across the azure afternoon and lets it fray

for those who stay here beside the wide estuary,
with otters and wildfowl pictured in the parlour
as a sign of peace. Three mallard fly up the stairs,

snipe and woodcock are copied onto crockery,
an amateur sun is framed in my cousin's hall
and she says, 'Come in,' in the accent I know well.

2 IN WEST LIMERICK

My Latin primer was like a prayer book at
Grandad's wake. I read *amo, amas, amat*
to myself dutifully. The country people sat

around me drinking porter or tea, while outside
the pile of towels burned poorly because of the rain.
Noreen's eldest was in the middle of exams

and Joe's last prayer that night would help the boy succeed.
'If you have any faith at all . . . ' I was left to
learn the verb *to love*. Before they closed the coffin

I was told to put down my book and look at him
in the room. He was the wit of Islanddanny,
Joe Walsh. He had heard the shots of Gort a' Ghleanna,

he had known a woman who'd been through the famine.
Then the men carried the coffin down to the road
on a wretched evening with soot-black clouds.

I remember how the coffin handles glowed
through the twilight, like the golden bough Aeneas
carried to the underworld. That was a few years

later, Book VI of *The Aeneid*, the hero's
quest with the Sibyl from Cumae, the winning steps
through a grammar that's remote and elemental,

like my first memories of an old man in his seat:
me biting into an apple he had given me
and then him asking, 'Well, boy *bán*, is it sweet?'

3 RIVER-TOWN

The first town-planner was a Dane wading the ford.
He conceived of a river dividing people
in that bare place, and gave to Lax weir its meaning.

Water was always going to be a concept here,
as was stone lifting grey stone above the river.
Anglo-Normans, Elizabethans, Cromwellians,

all kept the town's portcullis, but they died elsewhere
and left memories to the local historians
for them to celebrate the sullen garrison

and the gaudy jades in the streets of Irishtown.
They survive in an engraving under Turner skies,
these characters hidden by their burdens

as they unload the yawl at the wharf, the shawled women,
the ragged urchins, the tight waistcoat of the boss
who told the artist to make him look prosperous.

And then, later, there's this scene at Barrington's Pier
with young lads jeering at a Finnish timber-ship
as it surges proudly on its way from Limerick

before I was ready. So there I am, waving,
being abandoned to my early books on rivers:
the Volga, by Gorky; the Vistula, by Grass.

4 A STONE'S THROW

Released to the summer sea, we played skimming stones.
Each small discus hit eight, nine, or maybe ten times
before it faltered. We threw in the direction

that the planes were headed, taking off from Shannon
with their privileged set returning to the States.
We knew our station then, and used fragments of slate

or other well-shaped bits of stone for our scansion.
If you angled well on a calm stretch of water
you could extend the count to the syllables in

the British Overseas Airways Corporation,
that alexandrine along the length of the plane
we waved to the day Paddy went back to Boston.

He threaded the first path my stones were longing for
to America, to see myself checking in
with words to make the stone take off as metaphor.

5 A TRIP TO THE CAPITAL

The geography of the provinces was easy:
the towns made solid shoes and produced bacon
to supply the homes of a plain, frugal nation.

We knew this passing the stink of the pig factory
on our journey to Dublin via the station.
After three hours by train it was our history

we were meant to contemplate at the GPO
in Cuchulain's bronze body hanging from a tree.
Then, Ireland was a scruffy chiffchaff in a case,

it was an enormous whale's skeleton in mid-air
at the Museum of Natural History,
but it could live too at the Botanic Gardens.

I couldn't sleep the first night because of sirens
and the excitement of being a family
in a guesthouse, translated into a new place.

Next day, as we practised a stroll down Kildare Street,
just the four of us, we had strayed into a light
that was older than those national institutions,

and we're still walking in that Palladian space,
my father with his clumsy, deferential steps
forever strange to the proud city's etiquette.

6 EEL-BOYS

At high tide, nothing that happened could motivate
us, except the moment when an eel began to bite,
so we watched the tip of our rods for the slightest

tremor. That seismic event under the surface
would register in our gear, then we would reach, strike
and haul in the reluctant eel. The place we came

from was reflected in the burnished evening flood,
King John's thirteenth-century walls, two cathedrals
for the main denominations, a fishing rod

engaged with the contortions of a twisting fish
that landed, and then snaked it all over the road.
And this was the moment the tourist coaches slowed

to watch us, and take pictures. We were genuine
Irish, although the slime that came off on our hands
as we removed the hooks was hardly picturesque.

But they were satisfied. More snaps for the book
of photos making us immortal in New York
or Boston. We were the eel-boys who stole the show.

(Much more interesting than that boring Treaty Stone
on everyone's itinerary.) The eels took
until the tide turned, and the rippling Shannon

took the latest freight of pictures to the sea-bed
from the mirror of the river: the rapt faces
of the Americans and our wavering heads.

7 THE BOOKS IN MY ROOM

The shelves beside my bed were filled with Catholic
tradition: Belloc's essays beginning with On ——— ;
the detective stories of G K Chesterton;

some books by Douglas Hyde (a former Communist,
not the Frenchpark rector's son), one called *I Believed*;
Teilhard de Chardin in dialogue with Darwin;

Jacques Maritain; Christopher Dawson; Graham Greene.
I thought they explained the world and banished evil
in those black-and-white years after the war. London

had no appetite for experiment, and Waugh
was perfecting his snobbery in the country.
Freud was dead and Auden in the States. (The tall

figure of Eliot, out for his lunchtime stroll,
would call at the shop to see if his books had sold.)
So I slept with an élite that were not gentry

but had their own destructive ways, all of a kind
in this, that they darkened my room with a lifeless,
patronizing, intolerant Catholic mind,

until the day I picked up *Crime and Punishment*
in a shiny new paperback. Orthodoxy
was challenged in the name alone. Dostoyevsky

was a window on the prospects a Tsar had built.
I read eagerly along with Raskolnikov
and moved in his freedom on streets paved with guilt.

8 HOME

Was it the same as 'origin', the notion 'home'
in Pater's elegant prose? Once they had refused
the empire, we all had to make it on our own

with the precedents we knew: Auntie May's small house
on a dozen rushy acres near Abbeyfeale
where I spat my pure white toothpaste out the back door;

or Paddy's place at Inch, with its guard of greyhounds.
I wondered if I'd have the skill to throw a ball
down the biggest dog's throat to stop it barking.

Like Cuchulain, I wanted to roam the orchard
where a chaffinch was nesting, and walk the low wall
between the apple-trees and the mud of the yard

and not sit with the relatives in their boredom.
My mother thought that my uncle had it hard.
Maybe he would have been better off in London

where she had lived and met my father. Wood Green.
The Strand. A room in Notting Hill. The honeymoon
in Bournemouth. Trafalgar Square some fine afternoon

where Hannah, Beta and Noreen fed the pigeons.
'Why didn't you stay? The boss offered you a house.'
'No, London was no place to have children,' she said

firmly. So it was back to Limerick's lesser gain
on our account, not quite that 'undisputed place'
but what you say when you're asked, 'Where do you
    come from?'

Flieger Hartmann

It's nineteen sixty-nine,
and I'm following instructions,
sprawled out on my bed
making two model planes,

a Messerschmidt and a Hurricane
in perfect scale, with rivets,
and features on the pilots
sitting in the cockpits.

Hanging from cotton thread
pinned to the ceiling
between the wallpaper and the curtain
they fought the Battle of Britain

while I slept safely.
Give or take thirty years,
at a hilltop on the coast,
you reach a numbered sector

where ÉIRE shouts
its innocence in stone.
Then I hear Flieger Hartmann
in his plane, the drone

increasing with those familiar
rivets, and that frozen face
comes into view
behind the cockpit's glass.

Speaking his language
I can say he's come too far,
that Erris means no profit
and no threat to the Führer.

I could even manage to say
we're a less-than-serious race,
that his Luftwaffe cross
has no purpose in this place,

rehearsing the bit part
left over from the war,
the scene a western beach
where I play an islander

waving to the plane,
feeling flattered by the event,
and deflated when he lands
to face internment.

Two Sculptures by Gerald Müller

I DOLPHIN BARGE

Set on its block of oak,
the iron hull is economical
like the flat blade of a sled,
its toe a Persian slipper.

Faceted from the hammer,
the two upright nails
are muted figures
in proportion to the still vessel.

Between them, skewering
both their hearts,
the spit supports a mast
and a sail of dolphin bone.

All their pain can take
is this white apron
bellied amidships
tugging at their stake.

Aft, the smaller upright
could be the tiller,
but that open hole
in its body must mean

that it too is destined
to house something
like the sharp bar
in the chests of the couple.

And before you ask
'Who are these?'
notice the perfection
of their anonymity.

Think of Ulysses
determining his life
when he drove the pole as Nobody
into the Cyclops' eye.

2 AFRICA BARGE

Another skiff,
light as a kayak,
another standing couple.
A blunt instrument

has been abstracted
out of the man.
His features are two hollows
like the notches on a *bata scór*,

so he figures as two
infringements that the forger
has punished with sharp blows
between hammer and tongs.

More blows to the head
of a heavy nail
shape the straw helmet;
more to the body

make a tunic
beaten out for a woman.
The only flattery
is her lunula of bone.

Now she must stand
demurely in the shadow
of her man's shoulders
to be transported.

The boat proceeds
into the Bight of Guinea
past the tin shacks
of the trading station.

The picture freezes,
but the chains continue
to sound after the smith
has put his tools down.

Gale Warning

after Günter Grass

The storm blew from the west after a gale warning.
No dead this time, but many fallen trees,
damage to property, and fears of global warming
compounding our general unease.
This wide world has us jaded. Will we be able
to stay the course at the rich men's table,
or will our stocks come tumbling down
if this uninvited weather stays in town

to make itself at home? — like the foreign flood
that have the gall to want to mix their blood
with the fair, unblemished bodies of this state
so that we have another, not ourselves, to hate.
More storms are forecast for the coming nights.
They know no bounds, they knock, and demand their rights.

Horses at Corratowick

The horses were a surprise to the man,
a group of five with a foal on the flank of a hill,

standing dense at the gate
in the brown dough of ground

they had kneaded under a tree.
Whereas the man understood other steeds and horsemen,

these ones stayed
in the naked harness of mid-winter.

They rested at the source of steaming air
and had no mind for smashing branches then

or the next morning,
when he came back with the camera's eye.

They were too small to take
unless he got in with them

by climbing the bars of the gate
and getting their view of the back of a farmhouse.

So he staggered
on the broken slope as it fell into the valley,

taking him close to themselves,
but they didn't enthuse for the god of the sugar-cube —

they were grazing another peace,
their mouths welded to land,

their own vital organs
packed inside like Greek soldiers.

The buff stallion
dressed up the leaves of his ears at the whirr of the shutter,

a mere wren of a click,
not a man shouting with a black plastic stick,

or a man checking a fetlock.
The stallion drifted away to join the others

as the man watched them
with his naked eye,

until the mindless horses won
and the man twitched on.

The Helmet of Messapus

After the rites for Maurice Fitzmaurice
(his cold body splashed into the cold sea)
they sailed into Blacksod and cast anchor
at Fahy, under the massive bulk of Achill.
Water was needed, and fresh meat for the crew,
and the bravest were keen to explore the new country.
Avancini was the first to ask Alonso
if he could take fifteen chosen men
in two runs of the currach they had stolen
to go ashore. This man was impatient.
He was a tamer of horses schooled in cavalry,
and was mad for action. He chose liverymen,
horse-tamers like himself, to make the crossing,
and before he climbed down into the cockboat
he left the helmet of Messapus as a pledge
for his return. Then they fixed the oars;
they pulled hard on the oarlocks, and the light boat
went surging steadily towards landfall.

Euralo also wanted action. He said to Nico,
'I hope he feeds the monsters in that desert,
Mister Cock-of-the-Walk and his condottieri.
He thinks now we'll all be kissing his ring
when he comes back, but I'd sooner starve.'
Euralo and Nico, the two friends,
still hungry turned in again to sleep
for another night, as the ship dragged its anchor
and creaked in the rush of subsiding waters.
When they woke to another full tide
Euralo could hardly be contained
with his pit of hunger and frustration,
but Nico, the older man, held him.
'Don't go off at half-cock now.
If Avancini makes it, and the place is safe,
we'll all prosper. Otherwise we'll upstage him.

Wait.' So wait they did, on a sea
of grey water which wasn't their poetry.

The evening tide filled to the silent shore.
'Something's wrong,' Euralo said. 'There's no signal
after all these hours. Let me and Nico
go before the tide starts falling again.
We can swim across with empty barrels
and bring the cockboat back. You command.'

No sooner had he got the slightest nod
than this fiery young man rushed down
into the hold for two empty casks
and on his way back he hid the helmet of Messapus
in one of them without being seen.
So, clutching the casks they swam the water
to the shore with their teeth chattering,
Nico and Euralo, the two companions.
They came out in a creek near the cockboat.
Then Nico said, 'Let's get out of here.'
He was already pulling at the boat's rim
when Euralo, the young blood, stood
there suddenly, wearing the bronze helmet.
'What? You mean we just paddle back
to the ship like two hungry fishermen?
No way. You're the one who taught me
to fight for everything, Nico. Don't opt
out now.' Already Euralo
was headed for the ridge above the beach,
like the son who has his schooling from his father
and has grown to rival him in skill, if not in tact.
So wisdom followed youth, reluctantly,
until Nico felt the old fire
of action warming his thighs, shaking him
as the footsoldier shakes before a battle.

There was a castle visible not far off
which drew their interest. On the way
they quartered an old man's hovel
and took his food at knifepoint, and sat there
until dusk. Euralo would have stabbed him
to quench his blether, but in the end he was spared
when Nico said, 'It's a prime cut we're after,
not old meat.' The two men laughed
the laughter of old comrades.
                              When dusk had thickened,
the Italians slipped out onto the track
to check the approach to the castle. Then they vanished
back into the bog. This was their best option,
the wind would cover the sound of their plashing feet
as they crept up on the sentries. Euralo
muzzled the first with his hand. The man was strong
under the wrap of a heavy tweed mantle,
like a bony calf that won't be held for tagging,
so they struggled until the blade found the neck
and he sighed a little moan assenting to death.
Nico stabbed the other deep in the ribs,
but the man groaned loudly. 'Let's go!
Now! They'll be on us after this,' Nico hissed,
so he and Euralo scuttled back off the track
into the cover of the black bog. They were breathless,
and mad that their escapade might be cut short —
'No! Let's wait!' said Euralo.
'How do you know they've heard? Maybe not.'

The night was blowy and uncertain. The two men
were crouched in a nowhere within earshot of the castle.
They could hear laughter and see faint torchlight
in the window, but no alarm was raised
for the two others whose life went cold at the road.

Again, Euralo wanted to go on, but Nico
demurred. 'OK, you stay
but I'm going to find out if Avancini's
in there. You wait.' So the young man
harried into the darkness with his proud helmet
and left Nico waiting for a long time.
When he came back Nico could see that he
had been killing, the way he gasped
for breath and stammered, 'Yes, they've got them.
We'll have to go back and tell Alonso.'

As they believed the only danger lurked
at the castle, Nico and Euralo now emerged
back onto the track they had taken
just as the clouds were blown clear of the moon.
Three furlongs farther back, a party
of mounted soldiers was approaching Doona Castle
with the news that Sir Richard Bingham was headed
that way to capture anyone who landed
from the Armada ships. One of them spotted the helmet
gleaming in the moonlight, and shouted on, as if
to one of their own, but the two Italians
knew this was danger, so they made for the coast again
and that long kesh above the beach that would take
them back to the cockboat. Now
the Burkes sensed they were dealing with intruders,
so one of them galloped down to the sea on his pony
to cut off the shoreline. Others dashed
forward to surround the low ground at the coast
and complete the circle at the far end of the beach,
like the net that fishermen pull across a river.
Then they turn and row back rapidly
to the bank they came from, narrowing the noose.

These men were hunters, expert in this sport,
but they hadn't spotted Nico, who kept down
below the level of the kesh and crept along
the way a sparrowhawk follows the line of a hedge.
It was Euralo who got bogged down in mud
farther in where the ground was darker and unsure.
The first rider had seen him, and sped past
Nico, shouting *'Thall ansin! Ansin!'*
The saltmarsh was sliced up in deep trenches,
with steep banks and treacherous slippery margins.
Euralo couldn't distinguish the ground,
so he floundered there in his fear, with raw panic
exploding in his chest. Nico could have run.
As they closed in on his young friend, tears
flooded his face and an inner voice cried,
'What hope is there for you now,
Euralo? Braveheart. Youngblood.
How could I restrain you, and you set on mayhem!'
What was Nico to do, with one stabbing-sword
against several riders with spears and halberds?
But he couldn't leave the young man in the marsh
at the end of their spears, so he crept back
and stalked up on one of the riders who knew
nothing until Nico's steel knifed into his side.
The man screamed as Nico struggled with his horse,
to hold him in the hope of getting on,
but another rider rounded on him and struck him
in the shoulder with a halberd. Then he fell,
to be struck repeatedly, fatally in the head.
Euralo fought in a last attempt to scorn
his fate, but he too was slaughtered there,
his rib-cage trussed by two mounted spears.

                                              Nico and Euralo,
your lives ebbed and chilled in that gloomy night

remote from your Tuscan skies! Your style died,
and all your chivalry was wasted, lost
like the helmet of Messapus, stripped from Euralo's
body and exchanged from spear to spear by the horsemen.
Later it was stolen by a fool who planted it,
as he said, under the full moon.

Knock/Stansted

It comes true at last, the vision
of a great white queen of heaven
as definite as the monitors foretold.

She descends in her fabulous ruff
to chat to her uniformed captain —
and will not tolerate a smoker's cough.

It's a price they pay for the steady smile
that saves them from the destiny of ferries,
for the catwalk of her outfit for the sea,

now unlikely, as the country falls away
and the past becomes a miniature
to those who prosper up here too

with the star-trek signs and the blue
conviction that the sky should be
this happy colour, as of right.

But life is also weather on the ground.
The hostess has a home. She can't be famed
forever. The dream goes down,

as migrants must, while they still protest
in accents ringing from the homeland,
to plant both feet in Essex.

Furze in Wind

Early in spring, the furze goes wild in the wind,
its bright yellow flouting the laws of weather.
When the hills and bare trees risk nothing
before April, these loyal team supporters
pack the hillside.
                    This is one they have to win,
a vital away-game for Whin United!
If they miss the curlew they've lost everything.
And they don't need fame to get excited.
Happy in this amateur-drama sea,
they rear up, exult, and immediately
are dragged back into their substance.

Then the season ends for the revelling whins.
They drift as smoke in the hazy distance,
and the migrants sing beside the silent bones.

Summer

So we were all eyes at the window-eyes
as we scanned the hedges for their story.
It was mid-winter, and we improvised
with beds on the floor and borrowed deckchairs.
Then we found the rudiments of the year,
the golden saxifrage and strawberry
flowering precisely in Lugnafahy.

The nearest spring gave a rhyme of water,
the element changing clear containers
into twin loads of brightness unconstrained
from well to table.

                    When a dog took off
cross-country, over the next field, a man
followed along the road calling 'Homer!
Homer!' The place answered to the summer.

Other Forms

No sooner built than the house becomes a space
for other forms and signatures, new writing
like a spider on fresh plaster. A field-mouse
was the first to try the loft for a haunting,
and now a door left open on a May night
admits a different alphabet of insects.
Some fly against a window of regret
for what happened. Others poise like Stoics
on a frame. On floors and window-boards, a litter
of limping ones and stragglers drag their wings
in the after-glare of the next morning.
Airborne in a room they drift, the demure;
these flies deny that a house doesn't yield,
while they remain in this resolute let in the field.

The Previous Owner

The locals talk when they see the agent's sign
'FOR SALE', translating life into hearsay,
how he never really tamed the garden,
all that travelling, all those weeks away.
The townland watched his star as it fell wide —
and is falling still — of the style he wanted,
to strike his image in the countryside
forever, like a rebel or a landlord.

In fact, he was so transformed by nature
that the wildlife took over his whole mind
with its beautiful, indifferent data,
until he had to move, and leave behind
this house, still shining in the perfect tense,
while the owner's story takes him somewhere else.

A Souvenir

After the drive I was newly hatched from the car
and stood in the village centre, reading the signs
for the craft shop, the gallery, the B & B.

Of course I knew it was all a great improvement
on the hovels that inspired the trendy designs
on machine-knit sweaters and chunky pottery

but it wasn't what I came for. Where was the space
that no one advertised, the barest elements
of a native tradition that isn't for sale?

So I walked beyond the church and turned right into
an untarred bog road where the tyre-tracks faded out —
it felt like abandoning an exhibition —

and soon I was moving along a grant-aided
fence above a wall decorated with foxglove.
But scenery was still an icon. I hadn't yet

managed to find that witness I wanted to hear:
the nibbling sheep, the gorse, and even the débris
of the unofficial dump were there insisting

that the blether of an older language was lost
to the high-street vernacular that we prefer,
and they gave this landscape its peculiar silence.

Then the mist blew in, like those masses of vapour
that your plane passes through on the way down home. You
reluctantly leave unclouded sun for your place

of seasons; and your sight is enclosed, and you wait.
So I kept walking slowly until a break came
in the mist, and again the vista was restored

across the open bog. I could see fodder bags
from the salmon farm full of turf, and then I heard
a distant tractor, and when more of the mist cleared

I found myself in the middle of the workings.
It was strange to walk no-man's-land between trenches
where history had given way to sphagnum moss

in the abandoned sections; but some were still fresh
from a man's energy, and there he was, hoisting
the heavy portions of the long winter evenings.

'The starlings are flocking!' I said. 'The year must be
on the turn.' He still kept on cutting rapidly
with his eye on the work, having heard me alright

as I knew from a twist in his features. 'The night's
drawing in.' This was his first concession to speech.
And then, looking up for the first time: 'You've to fight

for everything you get in this life.' 'What about
the stories you told, and the language you mastered?
Was that not washed up for free one day on the beach?'

'Bad cess to it anyway. They had me pestered
morning, noon, and night. Kelly, Flower and the
    Norseman.
Nach raibh mé tinn tuirseach ag freagairt ceisteanna.'

'*Deirtear nach ualach é le hiompar.*' 'Maybe not
for you, but I was hardly tackled on the road
with the ass and panniers when they were on me.'

He was cutting again. Now this time, as each sod
fell on the heather above him, a challenge grew
to identify me as one of his seekers;

and sure enough the question came: 'What do you do
for a living? You have the look of a teacher.'
My first reflex was to contradict him — 'That's true,'

I said, and I thought of those harrassed recruits who
staggered into their first *naomhóg* at Dunquin Pier
and had never again been able to steady

themselves until they left again after a year
or two of trying to resist the spoiling sea.
'Maybe you understand what it was like to be

word list, storybook and boatman for everyone,
and still to have to fish. Every time I set out
the day at sea was unforseeable for my boat;

and like the first oar in the sound was how I wrote,
tentative, but I knew I should be travelling.'
I was cautious to spoil this by more questioning.

'You said it was grand to hold a book of your own.'
'Sea, a mhic. Sin rud amháin nár ghoid an aimsir.
An dtuigeann tú mé? Sin rud amháin a mhaireann.'

'And still, the book, you know, it's only one version.
The authorized version.' Then I laughed at the joke
which came between us. This he didn't need to know

and didn't try to fathom; not out of his depth,
but out of his milieu he'd known instinctively
when to steer back home and when the boats should follow

the glinting sea for mackerel. 'Well, I've had my say.
A life's only written once. Let others match it
if they can, but they won't get any more from me.'

The low cloud blew into the space dividing us,
so I shouted, 'We still read it as an example!
To find in the style of your life a proper style,

in all the styles' — but the air was thickened by mist,
so I couldn't see him.
                          And then he was gone.
It felt like time for me too to be getting on.

Bertra

At the end of the day waves are tired.
The beach has been rinsed of its opinions,
and that dog now racing over the shore
will deprive it of even its shorebirds.
The place is guarded by planning controls
that the bay and the mountains adhere to,
and once you skirt the fence around the dunes
you're alone, keeping pace with your shadow.

That shadow, ready to float forever,
is held back by your footsteps as you search
for parallels among the tones of clay,
marram grass and shingle. Like you, it stops
at the cork dried out like last year's apple,
the yellow bulb forgetful of its use,
the brush worn to abstraction from the surf —
but fragments like these are never enough.

None of this jetsam could ever cohere
like the double pendulum of your stride
where regret is even with indifference,
and the arrogance of blind conviction
alternates with a smile that sues for peace.
Either way, you still enact a passing
that's not the dog claiming an empty shore
or the seabirds either, which have to fly.

This evening you've come alone, so there'll be
no photographs of you in the landscape
beside an emotional sea. Nothing
will distract from the ordinary fact
of a man out walking during peacetime
in a style you've often admired, so slight
as he diminishes in the distance
and is almost lost in thickening light.

PART TWO

To Connacht

1

Not having read him yet, we still read on and he
wakes up out of everything he has forgotten.
He's now proving that memory doesn't have limbs,

nor is it the urge to stretch up tall and be called
by February sunlight to the bright window
where the moving limbs of the ash-branches

are unadorned. Like some untaught instinct stirring,
he pulls on his cords, girds the strap of his belt
and goes downstairs to the kitchen to make coffee

(strange, we share that impulse too). The crockery gleams
on the shelf. The pine table rests in the plane
of itself. His arm reaches for the coffee-jar

and relaxes back into its own completion
when he has grasped it. He sips, and the light sharpens.
The shadows of a dancing tree criss-cross the wall.

2

He crosses through nature on blustery mornings
from door to door, in the few hasty steps taken
from his house to the haven of the silent car.

The key rises to the cleft of the ignition
instinctively; it's how he unlocks the canvas
of fields and hedges from their failure to question.

Then a slight shuddering and a rasp of anger
announce the powerful magic of this era as
the new day is conjured in one unthinking stroke.

3

Everything ahead is angled on the steering:
the cold hillsides and stone walls, the bungalows and
cantering herds veer steadily to his command,

because this is now the real motion of the world,
this confident ribbon laid over the drumlins.
It cements the old trail taken over the fen

of first alders, into the intimate thicket
of willows, and then back up the hillside when
the old drovers and their herds climbed through the
    meadows.

Matthew is secure from the highwayman's arrow.
He's gliding through a landscape with the sound turned off,
past an old oak that used to serve as a gallows.

4

As he drives along, the roadsigns play cautious cards.
Nothing can come unprepared, but even these are
enduring symbols he feels called on to transform,

varicose bends where he arrows and is unsure
so he hugs the road, but the celandines are what
he really loves on the undisturbed bank above.

The black crucifix on a yellow background says
sunlight in the afternoon, the Messiah alone
in a litter of cans and abandoned programmes.

Then Orpheus appears in his legendary car
going down the steep incline of the black triangle,
only to lose it all in the rear-view mirror.

Despair drives his car off a pier into the sea.
That quaint steam train with its irresistible load.
That rampant stag in the moment he leaps the road.

5

He has sworn many times that 'wormy circumstance'
had no right to confine the flow of the driven.
And yet here are circumstances that can sustain

him as he sets out past the hard, triumphant sign
announcing *M4 (West)*. This is the vast ocean,
but it doesn't appear as a destination.

Not in the Pale, not on the Mullingar bypass
where the cars move under the bridge's single span.
Each further town has its grey spire, like the tower

of a ship on a journey through prosperous seas.
Here he feels the skies opening to Edmund Burke's
sublime of tall clouds and cautious husbandries.

He crosses the Shannon into the old offence.
The flooded pastures announce that the greater guilt
belongs in the weather, whatever the language. Then

past the sign for Mayo, meaning the highway moves
to match his wide designs and the late March day ends
with sunlight flaring on the potential bay.

6

In January, cow parsley, holly and furze
are enough for winter's monstrance. These make one arm
longer than the other when he arrives back home.

On St Brigid's Day, he's busy in the corner
of a field, gathering rushes into a batch
that used to have a purpose like a roof to thatch,

the long stalks piled up on the ground side by side.
Somewhere in his mind a pattern overlaps.
After two false starts he plaits the bright new year

to stand over the hearth as a regular cross.
The same day the cameraman memory snaps
Hanna moving in the sunlight in several shots,

and Matthew sitting at a door with rushes and
twine, managing to get the knack of real weft.
He stands up to look. He is pleased with his success.

7

Like the classical Hibernia the sculptor
made, the first of April inspires a legendary
matron with a catching laugh. This is what she says:

'Go on, put on the cap and bells, and paint yourself
a fixed smile of merriment. Today is Fools' Day
and the wild geese are laughing. They'll soon be back to

their business in the Arctic, not playing aero-
planes for the fun of dogs and galloping children.
The choppy sea is giddy in the afternoon sun,

and the gardens are full of jestering daffodils.
You can be the jeering genius of the place, light-
footed as Hermes, dashing off towards the bright

woodland which has not had enough time to pull on
her green dress. She's wearing only pussy willow.
She says, "Let's have fun before love gets serious."

Why should you, with your sad pace, stoop to lower life
across the barren strand, enquiring after forms,
gloomy as a crustacean? The sea's border lace

is spilled in mirth. Today the sun hatched in the west
and by noon she will have pushed out your metaphors
like a young cuckoo in a meadow pipit's nest

and expect you to feed her up fat and hearty.
This thing you conceived is growing like nothing you knew,
and the joke's on you, the tired entertainer.'

8

Taking a flinty ridge out of the pastoral,
the quartzite rises above the map-maker's road
with its gatherings of sheep, like famine victims.

At the trig point on the searing, open summit,
Matthew is reminded of Lear's metaphysic
as he reads *Maura* and *Cian* in the lettered stones.

He could brood too long on a technicality,
in terms of absence (no dotterel or ptarmigan).
But Hanna is right to insist on getting home.

And they desert, like ants in their own tiny scale
progressing down a boulder, with the setting sun
falling into the distant, grey, jostling sea.

Getting back to the car is a return to life
as they know best. Everyone agrees. The nicest
thing after a ramble is a 'hot cup of tea'.

9

The locals know that the house is rented again,
but the car-owners see very little of each
other in the winter and they keep to themselves.

A man is seen crossing the wide bowl of the glen
like a spider in the bath of their suspicion,
but they avoid him. A dog arrives in the night

instead, to sniff at the rubbish, and rip open
the plastic bag holding evidence of the past:
tea-bags dissolving the ink of private letters,

milk cartons, tins, leftovers and cardboard pictures,
Alpine packs advertising muesli, a box that
still bore the promise of a pizza out of Tuscany.

10

One morning Matthew drives down to the sea. He knows
that others would come after him, wanting to know
what had taken him there, because spring invites him

to an easy chair overlooking the valley,
where God is hoisting the skylarks on their pulleys
into the bright air and taking all the credit.

The waves are off on other business and they keep
the crabs and seagulls waiting on the exposed banks
where they can watch out for the promise of full tide.

And then, a man who seems to have nothing to hide
walks out over the beach to ask the same question
of the coast, and is followed by his printed stride.

Where is the future tense? Where is the present?
So I write now, and now, to each of his lifted
feet with the slightest heave of the wet element

in the sand, and just as the sole falls, the surface
that has been perfected this morning in the ebb,
the surf now fallen, like paper under a nib,

will be waiting for the driver thudding his door.
Watch him now, as he combs along an empty beach
and reaches the shingle to pick up a spent flare.

11

It was partly bedrock and partly myth that built
the national route taking both of them through the heat —
that foreign country — from the dour clays of Connacht

to the sweeter stone farther south. Once, a black cat
started at an opening in the hedge and darted
back into furtive nature in the undergrowth.

On these journeys, if the outcome is uncertain,
the onward motion has a substance of its own
as you hold to your own line in the left-hand lane.

Galway's northside is as depressing as ever
but by Kinvara the tide of expectation
is filled by the oncoming hills of bare limestone.

The landscape consents to Yeatsian illusion,
a native Renaissance with dream thorn and dream rock
before Robert Gregory changed his painter's frock

for a pilot's uniform. So the objects ask
them for a comment on the same stones and trees.
The pub they avoid is the one called *Raftery's*.

12

While the other two drive, Kevin sits in the yard,
determined, with hazel rods and a sharpening blade,
to keep chickens from the plot with a palisade

of spears and wire; Jane finds some peace in the garden,
thinning lettuces or tying the onion stalks
like unruly daughters who would never be said;

with Michael slung under her like a sail, she walks
the rows she planted in April when the sky was
still spinning on the potter's wheel of breezy days.

The shavings from the hazel-points are mileage told
as Matthew and Hanna drive down a corridor
of the same trees, in little bodies, a small shoal

of wood cuttings being dropped from the pool of his blade.
'When did they say they'd be here?' 'About four o'clock,'
Jane says from the plot. 'But maybe they got delayed.'

Kevin stops sharpening to roll a cigarette
with the damp moss of shag tobacco, and his smoke
floats through the heavy air of hot weather set

in its blue sky above the rocks of Mullaghmore.
The garden is coming on, it makes a difference
to their pocket, with the kid now they need more

money; and if his honeybees get any chance
this year August will be good at Ennis market,
his grimy van full of their own home-grown produce.

He can see in some of the faces that he is despised
like someone who shunned the church on Sunday. But it
doesn't matter to him. Then the blue car arrives.

13

In their gifts they bring an edge of opulence, like
relatives from abroad. The rainbow-coloured, wool
dungarees for the little one, some malt Bushmills,

and a flank of smoked salmon, a prize from the sea
swollen with the strength of richer economies.
Jane and Kevin live a different geography.

Colombian coffee and Lebanese hashish,
incense-sticks made in India, patchouli oil,
different spices for the pans of vegetables.

'You can stay as long as you like. There's no sweat, man,'
says Kevin, looking to the garden — so his is
the brow that labour wouldn't moisten! Then, breaking

the leaves' silence: 'There's plenty of food. You've a room
to yourselves. It's comfortable in there.' 'It is . . . now,
at this time of the year,' Jane adds, somewhat bitterly.

And then: 'You should try sleeping in there in winter!'
'Winter's winter,' says Kevin philosophically,
as he breathes out smoke and takes a sip of coffee.

14

In the beginning there was a grove of hazel
trees extending in the sheltered lee of the hills,
and the sun rose and set over them in spite of

science teaching that our planet moved. Nowadays
the mainstream is confused. But most academics
would refuse if offered the drug psilocybin

by four friends on a verandah, around a table,
high in their own minds on the sun that is setting
reliably on aboriginal hazel.

Then Kevin drops the spar of a record needle
on the pulsing waves of the warped black plastic sea
and the air throbs with Bob Marley's identity.

The sky is darkening into a gentian blue.
With each reggae refrain they are counting the bats
as they come out from the eaves of the house and fly

out over the swarming leaves: thirty-six in all,
spinning in epicycles, like the ancient planets
keeping the strict laws of the schoolmen's ritual.

The way they talk you can tell they're educated
although they keep to themselves. What the locals hated
is the poverty, the clothes, the melancholy.

15

Today Matthew is sitting outdoors to create
with a sketch of drystone wall and a bluff of limestone
his absent self, a scene which will exonerate

him, with deliberate control, from mindless life.
He doesn't draw the second-hand van that Kevin
has bought from the County Council. He has had strife

with the engine this morning so the motor roars
when he tears past on his way to collect some gear
for a rock band in Ennis. And the exhaust pours

an incense that diminishes with the letters
on the van, *Leabharlann an Chontae*, on the side.
This doesn't appear in the sketchbook countryside.

Then Hanna and Jane intervene with a basket,
hunting the grassy patches for fly agaric
which was a poison, therefore a cure for something

that they are going to look up in the almanac
which Jane keeps on the shelf with the *Chinese Book of
Changes*, McGahern, and Tolkien's *Lord of the Rings*.

A cure for depression, for Michael's nasty cough,
for Kevin's foul humour in the mornings when he's
been drinking, or mixed drink with the other stuff.

16

Kevin is away, making music somewhere else,
so the record player is quiet. With Michael
under her, Jane works the garden like a creature.

The peace holds just the small sounds of preparing food,
pods clicking open to divulge stowaway peas,
the garlic a smart, urgent rattle on the board.

'Now where would I find a stock cube?' she asks the sauce,
whose lips bubble something that meant 'Feel free
to look in the cupboards,' as Kevin recently

insisted, 'Make yourselves at home.' So she peeps in-
to the shelves and drawers of foreign territory
and finds them beside the packet of black-eyed beans —

no, not the Oxo, the medical syringes
speaking a danger in nature in the tropics,
a devil's milk incised from the heads of poppies.

The steaming food comes to the table in Kevin's
absence. It is good and wholesome, so no one says
much before he gets back and is served his portion.

'Guess what. The Stokers broke up! I'm the transport for
the new band. I'll be driving with all the gear.'
Jane reads warning signs into his great good humour.

'If this works out, will I be doing the bees this year?'
'Why shouldn't it?' he says, spearing a potato
carelessly with a fork as if it were his life.

17

Near the house, at the acute angle of two roads,
Leabharlann an Chontae is parked under the foliage
of sycamores. A flycatcher hunts where trees make

shelter for flies to hover. A hound starts barking
at the end of its radius in the shadow
when another van pulls up. Despite the angry sounds

of doors being slammed and opened, the chaffinch's song
continues up in the canopy. Down below,
black boxes and a drum kit are being unloaded

from Kevin's van into the other van when he arrives.
'What the fuck do you think you're up to!' he explodes
at the other two. 'It seems you've taken the wrong

equipment, man.' They pause, while the bird sings on.
When one of them turns to unload another drum
Kevin pushes him from behind, so he turns on him

and gives him a wallop with his fist as the dog
goes crazy rearing up at the end of its chain.
Jane appears, screeching abuse at the two fetching

the rest of the equipment out of Kevin's van.
Then she becomes Pietà for her fallen man.
Paul and Dennis steer round the frenzied dog one last

time with the drumsticks, climb into the loaded rig,
and then start her up into a strangled reverse.
'We couldn't wait,' Dennis jeers. 'A supporting gig

in Athlone tonight. No time to negotiate.'
The van lurches forward out of the sycamores
into the midday glare. Weak glimmers penetrate

to where Kevin stands again. The dog still rears
up beside the woman in the yellow dapple
of an antique painting as the van disappears.

18

The scene is a house in the country with hazels
in the distance. Time: the present, in the evening.
A man, mid-thirties, paces up and down, and pulls

on a cigarette. He is wearing runners and jeans,
and seems preoccupied. Near him a woman stills
an infant she's holding in her arms and looks as

if she's been crying. She's cast as the figure
of grief and forebearance. A woman in a cream
suit and a man dressed in loose casuals appear

from the front. They both look the professional type.
They proceed straight up towards the verandah together
and then they separate as the woman takes up

a position sitting on the rail to the right.
Then she gazes towards her companion who stops
in front of the house. At first it seems that he might

join the first man who paces like a caged jaguar,
but instead he turns round to face the evening light
now concentrated at a point slightly higher

than where they entered. The four people in the frame
could be reliefs on an allegorical jar,
a scene held before release into the future.

19

A sudden shower of rain sprinkles the windscreen.
They're on the move again, with Matthew holding
the steering like some sedentary sea captain.

When he switches on the sirens of the wipers
they start to cry like an artwork installation
wiping its arms in supplication on the glass

and moaning 'Why? Why? Why?' in repeated question,
like the refugees who wash your window during
a halt in the traffic. The shower clears again.

'Wait until it's dark,' Kevin has told them. 'Then work back
from the Abbey. A hundred yards from the second
gate, on the right, there's an entrance. No one will see

you.' And no one did, when Matthew cancels the night-
leaves that flourish in the bright shaft of the headlights
by switching them off. He takes a torch from the boot

and beacons his way into the rhododendrons
where a woodland track is rumoured to take them both
to a dry, grassy space beside a disused kiln.

The torchlight paints in long, evaporating strokes
the setting he needs: the muddy track under oaks,
then the grassy space, and the old walls rising up

wherever the torch beam finds them in the darkness.
He startles a badger back into its black space
as he goes back to tell Hanna he's found the place.

20

At night-time in the wide cradle of the valley
there's another night-time inside the dreaming mind,
with sight asleep. The tent wall shudders in the wind

freshening through the wood as a rustling of oak leaves.
It's a dream, you see, so she doesn't challenge him
with 'Where are you going?' She can hardly worry

if only soul has deserted his sleeping form.
The dream takes him to a graveyard of useless cars.
There's a make called Zephyr. It's been dumped out of sight,

still proclaiming the worth of the English motor
and giving a British flavour to Connemara.
And Pallas is here too, with his boot open

and his name-badge askew in the shifting torchlight.
The name gleams like a coin offered to a ferryman
by another at a strange river, who's unsure

of the currency. He still manages to cross that moor
and comes to the graveyard. He approaches a car
lit from within by light originating in

the rear-view mirror. A person is seated
with his face lit by the same light, staring ahead.
Then he knocks on the glass to say he has arrived.

21

Matthew jests that his was a pedestrian death.
He senses that the shade is now beyond offence
and that he will lose nothing with this reference

to the car accident near the Collège de France.
'It was the lingering weeks I found the hardest,'
the voice answers in a curiously flat drawl.

Even the accent of pain sounds mechanical
but is painful nonetheless, as if the dead man's
voice is now embedded outside himself. And then

Matthew wants to ask him: 'So nothing we have seen
survives in what we say? Have I still got you right?
I'm thinking of those early months of the year when the
    green

of spring takes hold on the land. Is it archaic
to say it happens every time, although I lack
the words to say it as new as the leaves themselves?'

'It is not the season that we see, but the shape
of our own desire.' 'What about that little boy
in the photograph? You know, the one in the book

you wrote about yourself. Don't tell me you'll deny
him, with his fresh bonnet and he starting to walk
across the hot beach as Proust finished his *Recherche*.'

'I grant you that there's pathos there, but it's yourself
who turned to those early, summery photographs,
yourself in the tender moment of looking back,

and it was your hand that took the book from the shelf.'
'So?' 'Desire is easy in retrospect. It turns
into nostalgia for the thing that can't be done

because it's over. On the other hand, when it's
pointed forward from the here and now it unfolds
into the proud danger of its own fulfilment.'

'But the past in the mirror is the element
that lights your face.' 'That's only when a person's dead.
In your life it's a poor lamp for the road ahead

of you. Try to think of each pencil-stroke instead
as a mark that's hazarded into the unknown
and listen to the other self that you've become

in the motion of the scripting. Matthew, you are
alive. You stand on the borders of your own self
just as it's being delivered into something else.'

22

The dream is losing focus. With the day's pale tide
encroaching on the wall of the tent, he struggles
to follow Barthes as he drives up the mountainside

in the Citroën that has suddenly revived.
It shoots light onto the lonely rushes. Hanna
unzips the entrance of the tent without warning,

inviting the cool of morning to flood into
their sleeping folds. Day was where they would be doing,
with only intervals to court the dream memory.

'O Matthew, look at this!' she says to the first light
where the Twelve Bens appear now in the place of last night's
sky. The north crags are clear and still brisk this summer.

There are shreds of morning mist smoking around them
with the raven and fabled wren; from high ledges
above the silver capsule, mountain sheep look down

at two squinting heads coming out of their cocoon.
The campers speak a language completely unknown
to the watching creatures. It rises in volume

with their delight once they move free of the tangles
that had kept them warm. Almost out of their eyes' range,
a mated peregrine soars out of his eyrie

and in wide, spinning loops searches for his reflection
in the lake before it is touched by the humans
hatched from their star. Now they shout in the freedom

of the cold waters creeping up over their skin
and in the vast ripples spreading away from them
the peregrine loses his image in the surface.

So he glides off into something undetermined
by the beak of his circling pen. His final turn
describes their otter heads before abandoning.

Two Goodbyes

The first is contained inside
the second as memory.
You travel the open road
that still remembers their shy
Gaelic when the surface was
untarred. Then, in Ballina,
you ask where the station is,
because you're already far
from your familiar setting
as he was, boarding the train,
with a cake of bread in
his pillow case.
                        If he failed
to remember the changes,
a label on his waistcoat
gave details of his address
on the farm outside Glasgow.
The carriages that stand there
are emptied of that story.
(He's still at the open door,
surprised that they should worry
about him, at the urgent
grasp of his father's hands on
his.) Today, you are intent
on a train there for no one,
with a view across the seats
from the platform where you stand
to the growth of meadowsweet
on the embankment beyond
and, of course, your reflection
on the glass that now ripples
with the train set in motion,
and your own image vanishes
as a shiver in the leafage
of the siding.

Notes and Acknowledgements

page 15   *Abraigí anois é.* Say it now.

page 23   *Laidhrín.* Irish name for waders of the genus *Tringa*: redshank and greenshank.

page 38   Gerald Müller is a German sculptor and ironworker who lives in Rossport, a remote area of north-west Mayo.

page 40   *Bata scór.* A tally stick, used in the nineteenth century for recording the number of times school pupils broke the prohibition on speaking Irish.

page 45   This poem conflates the Nisus and Euryalus episode from Book IX of Virgil's *Aeneid* with events in Blacksod Bay, County Mayo, in 1588, when some ships of the Spanish Armada took shelter there. I have drawn on Rita Nolan's account of these events in her book, *Within the Mullet* (second edition, 1998).

page 49   *Thall ansin!* Over there!

page 57   *Nach raibh mé tinn tuirseach ag freagairt ceisteanna.* Wasn't I sick and tired of answering questions. *Deirtear nach ualach é le hiompar.* They say it's no load to carry.

page 58   *Sea, a mhic. Sin rud amháin nár ghoid an aimsir. An dtuigeann tú mé? Sin rud amháin a mhaireann.* Yes, son. That's one thing the weather never stole. Do you understand me? That's one thing that lasts.

page 80   *Leabharlann an Chontae.* County Library.

Acknowledgements are due to the editors of the following publications, where some of these poems have previously appeared: *Beyond the Reek* (Westport), *The Irish Times*, *Irish University Review*, *Metre*, *Poetry Ireland Review*, *Recorder* (New York) and *The Stinging Fly*.

I wish to thank Caitríona Hastings for help with some Irish source material.